Wok Cookbook for Beginners:

By Claire Daniels

The Top Easy and Quick Recipes for Wok Cooking For Beginners!

2nd Edition

Table Of Contents

Introduction

I want to thank you and congratulate you for purchasing the book, *"Wok Cookbook for Beginners: The Top Easy and Quick Recipes for Wok Cooking For Beginners!"*.

This book contains proven steps and strategies on how to cook delicious meals using your wok.

Basically, the book has three chapters. The first one tackles the general tips that you need to know when using the wok. The second chapter, the heart and soul of this compendium, contains the easiest wok recipes. Finally, the tips on how to clean your wok are discussed in the third and final chapter.

Thanks again for purchasing this book. I hope you enjoy it!

Chapter 1 – General Wok Cooking Tips

Before we jump into any particular recipe, you need to get the hang of using your wok first. Usually, the wok is used for stir-frying. Therefore, you need to learn how to stir-fry. Aside from being delicious, what is it with stir-frying that you would want to learn how to do it?

First and foremost, stir-fried meals are delicious. Aside from that, the resulting meals can be prepared fast. The meals are also really healthy and seasoned. Stir-frying with the use of a wok leads to the creation of meals that can lead to the creation of beautiful works of art in the form of good food. This method is best suited for making meals for one or two people. But if you will choose to cook meals for many people, this can be used, too.

Many people see the wok as an unattractive ornament in the kitchen. This notion is common among people who are not aware of the kinds of dishes that can be made from it. But many people are attracted instantly to have one once they tasted the dishes for themselves. Woks are essential for cooking authentic tasting dishes.

Here are some tips that are worth remembering:

Chinese Black tea, 2 whole star anise, 1 teaspoon of cornstarch, and 4 teaspoons of cold water.

In a large mixing bowl, whisk together the following ingredients: Chinese rice wine, soy sauce, 2 teaspoons of sugar, and minced ginger. This will be your marinade. If you are using a frozen salmon, make sure to thaw it properly first. After thawing, cut the salmon crosswise. It should be cut crosswise into 1-inch strips. Add the marinade and coat the salmon completely. Allow to sit for at least ten minutes.

Use a heavy duty wok for this recipe. Make sure to use a big piece of aluminum foil to line your wok. Allow the foil to hang over the wok's edge. In another bowl, mix the following ingredients: long grain rice, brown sugar, the Chinese Black tea, and the star anise. This will serve as your smoking mixture. Spread the smoking mixture at the bottom of the foil that serves as the lining of the wok.

Now, you may set a round rack around the mixture. It should be approximately an inch on top of the mixture. If needed, the aluminum foils should be scrunched into four balls. These should be placed on top of the mixture such that the wire rack can be properly elevated. The uncovered should be placed on high heat. Allow it to be there for the next five to

- It is worth purchasing your very own carbon steel wok instead of deep sauté pan. Aside from being very affordable, they are very versatile as well.

- Woks made up of carbon steel will have to undergo seasoning. The process of seasoning is not really difficult. This process can help your wok become better looking. It can also make your nonstick.

- The steps in the subsequent chapter may appear to be intimidating. But with consistent practice, you will find out that cooking in a wok is fun and fulfilling. Learn the recipes that follow by heart and be proud of the meals that you are about to produce.

Chapter 2 – Easy Wok Recipes

Wok Recipe #1: Stir-Fried Ramen

This meal will serve one to two people. The following are the ingredients that you need to prepare: classic ramen noodles and flavor, 2 tablespoons of wok oil, 1/3 cups of onions cut into strips, 1/3 cup of cabbage cut into strips, and 1/3 carrots cut into strips.

First, you need to cook the ramen noodles using the directions given in the package. Drain it and set it aside for a while. The wok oil should be heated up in a frying pan. Once hot, you may add the onions, followed by cabbage and the carrot strips. Once the veggies are cooked to perfection, you may add the noodles and stir it constantly. Upon heating the noodles, add the packet of flavoring. Stir the resulting ramen.

Wok Recipe #2: Shanghai Noodles stirred in a wok with Haricots Verts and Shrimps

This meal can be prepared in one hour, forty-five minutes for preparation and 15 minutes actual cooking. This recipe serves four to six people.

The following are the ingredients that you have to prepare: 1 pound of blanched and refreshed shanghai noodles (the one made out of eggs), ¾ pounds of blanched and refreshed haricots verts, 1 pound of rock shrimp, 1 tablespoon of cornstarch, 1 teaspoon of sesame seed oil, 1 teaspoon of coarse ground coriander seed, 1 tablespoon of minced garlic, 1 tablespoon of minced ginger, 1 piece of sliced red onion, ½ cup of sliced rehydrated black mushrooms, ½ cup of chicken stock, ¼ cup of oyster sauce, some canola oil, and black pepper and salt to taste.

Mix your shrimp, coriander, cornstarch, and sesame oil in a bowl. In a heated wok that is covered with just enough canola oil, you need to stir fry your shrimp for around two minutes until medium rare. The shrimp has to be set aside. In the wok, you need to add a little more canola oil so that you can caramelize your garlic, onions, and garlic. Then, you may season according to preferred taste. Then, you can add oyster sauce, chicken stock, and mushrooms. After that, you may add the noodles, the haricots, and the shrimp. Heat up as quickly as possible and serve immediately.

Wok Recipe #3: Noodles cooked in the Wok Stirred with New Year Veggies

This dish is traditionally served to represent long and unbroken life. It is traditionally eaten during the celebration of Chinese New year for good luck.

The following are the ingredients that you have to prepare: 1 tablespoon of vegetable oil and a bit more that will be used for frying, six to eight slices (around 1/8 of an inch thick) of lotus root, 1 teaspoon of chopped garlic, 1 teaspoon of finely-chopped ginger, 2 ½ ounces of Chinese celery that has been julienned into 1 ½ inches long pieces, 2 ounces of yellow leeks cut into 1 ½ inches long pieces, 2 ounces of sliced shiitake mushroom caps, 2 ounces of black trumpet mushrooms, 2 ounces of snow peas, julienned, 1 tablespoon of Shao Hsing wine, ¼ cups of chicken broth, 1 tablespoon of oyster sauce, ½ teaspoons of sugar, ¼ teaspoon of coarse salt, 8 ounces of e-fu noodles that has been reconstituted according to the directions of the package, 3 drops of white truffle oil, 8 to ten pieces of scallions that has been julienned carefully picked to include only the light green and white parts.

The wok filled with vegetable oil has to be heated until the temperature reaches 250 degrees Fahrenheit. The lotus root can then be added and fried until golden brown. This can be transferred to another bowl. You can wipe off the excess oil using the paper towel.

Then, you can heat another teaspoon of vegetable oil in a wok. Use high heat to cook your ginger and garlic until they are golden brown. Next, you need to add leeks, celery, mushrooms, broth, wine, and snow peas. You can proceed with cooking by stirring for the next thirty seconds. The mixture has to be transferred to a medium sized bowl. You can set the veggie mixture aside.

You may add chicken broth, salt, sugar, and oyster sauce to the pan. Then, you will need to add the noodles to cook. Toss the mixture constantly until all the liquid component of the mixture is absorbed. Let stand for about 1 minute. Return the veggies to the mixture and allow cooking. Aid this with constant stirring. Before removing from the heat, add truffle oil.

Serve while hot. You have the option to garnish your dish with scallions and the previously fried lotus root.

Wok Recipe #4: Scallop Salad in a Wok

The following are the ingredients that you need to prepare: 2 cups of fresh peas (sugar snap variety), 2 cups of spinach, 1 can (8 oz.) of water chestnuts, 2 pieces of shredded carrots, ¼ cup of olive oil, 1 pound of bay scallops, 1 tablespoon of tamari, 2 tablespoons of plum wine, 1 ½ tablespoons of sesame oil, 1 tablespoon of rice wine vinegar, 1 tablespoon of fresh ginger that is minced, and 1 ½ teaspoons of minced garlic.

First, you have to cook the peas in water that is already in full boil. Cover this for half a minute. To stop the process of cooking, drain and put water with ice. Then, you can add in the spinach, peas, shredded carrots, and water chestnuts into a large bowl. For a while, you can set this aside. The scallops can be cooked in hot olive oil using your wok. Use high fire in doing so. Turn the scallops once. Set this aside. Then, you can combine the tamari to the other ingredients. The vegetable can be drizzled over and tossed gently. You may top this with scallops.

Wok Recipe #5: Duck Fried in Oyster Sauce in a Wok

The skin of the duck should be properly scored. Place the duck with skin side down. Put it in a wok. Now, you may turn on the fire. Set it to high. Allow the duck to warm up slowly. By doing so, you will be able to extract the fat contained by the skin. By doing this for the next ten minutes, you will get a better flavor and texture.

On the other hand, you can boil a pot of water. Then, you can put in a dash of oyster sauce to the boiling water. Next, boil the pechay for around two minutes until it is wilted. Drain this and set this aside. Put the fire to low and cook for a few minutes more. After a while, remove the contents from the wok. Allow the duck to cool until it is cool enough to be handled and sliced thinly.

Pour 1 tablespoon of fat from the duck into the wok with the oil. Place the wok into high heat. Put the duck into the hot duck fat. Allow this to cook for the next three minutes until the duck is golden brown. Add pechay and oyster sauce. Simmer the mixture for around two minutes. Serve this while hot.

Wok Recipe #6: Wok-Fried Squid with Greens

This dish is very easy to cook. All you need is ten minutes of cooking time. The preparation of the ingredients will take you around the same time, too. This dish serves two to four people.

The following are the ingredients that you need to prepare: 2 tablespoons of olive oil, 1 pound of squid (including the tentacles and bodies) thoroughly cleaned and sliced into rings (1/2 inches thick), 1 ½ pounds of green leafy vegetables of choice (e.g. pechay), 2 pieces of finely diced Serrano chili, 3 cloves of garlic that are sliced very thinly, ¾ piece of grated ginger, 2 tablespoons of fish sauce, 2 teaspoons of brown sugar, 2 tablespoons of lime juice, and 1 ounce of basil (approximately three pieces of large stems).

The wok needs to be put on medium fire. Once the wok is hot enough, you may put one tablespoon of olive oil. When the wok is already smoking hot, you can add 1 tablespoon of olive oil. Sauté the greens until they are wilted for about five minutes. Set them aside. You may add more olive oil to the hot wok. Then, you add garlic, Serrano chili, and ginger. You can now add squid. Allow this to cook for around 2 minutes.

Mix the following: lime, brown sugar, and fish sauce. Then, you may add this to the greens that you have cooked earlier.

Sauté with the basil leaves until the basil is already wilted. Over barley or brown rice, serve the dish. The barley or brown rice will absorb the juices that resulted from the cooking process.

Wok Recipe #7: Fried French Beans and Carrots in a Wok

It is not right to conclude that just because this is made up of veggies, the resulting dish is no longer tasty. Try this and you will find out that the sweetness given by the carrots and the crunchiness provided by the beans will give you something that is heavenly. This recipe can serve 2 people.

The following are the ingredients for this particular dish: 200 grams of peeled carrots sliced on a particular angle, 200 grams of blanched and trimmed French beans, 1 tablespoon of ground nut oil, 2 cloves of finely chopped garlic, 1 tablespoon of oyster sauce, 1 tablespoon of ginger that is finely grated, 1 tablespoon of light soy sauce, 1 tablespoon of rice vinegar, and for garnishing, some crispy shallots.

This dish is fairly easy to cook. First, you just have to put the oil to the wok and set the fire on high. Then, you can cook the ginger and the garlic. You may cook this for thirty seconds.

The carrot can be added and it needs to be cooked for the next sixty seconds. You may add the beans together with the oyster sauce, the soy sauce, and vinegar. Toss this for the next thirty seconds. Serve while hot. You may top this with fried shallot as garnishing.

Wok Recipe #8: Chili Fried Chicken

Note that this recipe serves four people. The following are the ingredients that you need to prepare: 1 pound of chicken breast that has been cut into cubes (1 inch x 1 inch), 1 ½ cups of cornstarch, 2 teaspoons of salt, 1 teaspoon of ground black pepper, 3 cups of peanut oil or any vegetable oil, 8 to 10 pieces of dried chili, 3 cloves of minced garlic, 1 piece of leek sliced thinly (use the white part only).

For the marinade, prepare the following: 2 tablespoons of soy sauce, 2 pieces of egg whites, and 2 tablespoons of dry sherry or Chinese rice wine.

For the sauce, use the following: 2 tablespoons of garlic sauce with chili, 1 tablespoon of soy sauce, 1 tablespoon of water or chicken stock, 1 teaspoon of high quality balsamic vinegar (or more preferably, Chinese black vinegar), 1 teaspoon of cornstarch, and 1 teaspoon of ground Sichuan pepper.

You need to prepare the marinade first. In a bowl, you can mix in the following ingredients: rice wine, soy sauce, and the egg whites. The chicken should be coated with the mixture prepared for the marinade. Allow this to sit for at least ten minutes.

For the sauce, the following ingredients have to be mixed together: mix the soy sauce, the chili garlic sauce, the Chinese black vinegar, the chicken stock, the Sichuan pepper, and the cornstarch. This should be set aside for a while.

In a plate or a large bowl, you can mix the following seasonings: pepper, cornstarch, and salt. The chicken that was coated previously can now be dredged in this mixture. Shake the excess cornstarch off.

Next, you may heat three cups of vegetable oil or peanut oil in the wok. Let the oil heat up until it reaches the temperature of 350 degrees Fahrenheit. Fry the chicken in two to three batches. Fry the first batch of the cubed chicken breasts and fry these until they become golden brown. Make sure that they are cooked thoroughly inside and out. The entire process of frying can be finished within four to five minutes. The chicken can be removed with the use of a strainer to drain the oil. To remove excess oil, allow to drain in paper towels. Now, fry the second batch.

In a heatproof container, drain the oil. Save the oil for discarding. Wipe your wok with the use of a paper towel. If there are brown bits, remove them. However, it is not recommended to wash the wok.

Now, you may reheat the wok using high heat. Put in one tablespoon of oil. Swirl the oil so that the sides and base can be coated. You may add the dried chili to your wok and fry until they begin to blister. Stir-fry the ginger, garlic, and leeks. Now, you can add the sauce. Allow the mixture to thicken by allowing to boil for the next one minute. Finally, add the fried chicken. Toss this for thorough mixing, and the heat can be removed. This can now be immediately served.

Wok Recipe #9: Chicken Curry in a Wok

Note that for this dish to be successful, you have to use high quality curry. Many experts recommend curry in the paste form. This gives more depth and a richer kind of flavor compared to the more common curry in powder form. You need to be sure that you shake the canned coconut milk first because it has the tendency to have the creamy part float.

The following are the ingredients that you need to prepare: ½ teaspoons of vegetable oil, 3.5 pounds of chicken, 1 cup of shallots that are sliced thinly, 3 tablespoons of yellow curry paste (alternately, if you love the curry in powder form, you can use 1 tablespoon of curry powder instead), ½ cup of coconut milk in can (the unsweetened variety), ¾ cups of chicken broth, 2 potatoes that are peeled and quartered (cut into ¼ inch slices), 1 piece of green bell pepper cut into strips, 1 teaspoon of salt, and ¼ teaspoon of ground white pepper.

First, you need to heat a wok until the surface is almost dry. A good indicator for this is when the water beads in the wok vaporize within 2 seconds of contact with the heated surface. Now, you may put in the oil. Add the pieces of chicken with the skin side down. Spread this throughout your wok. For the next three to four minutes, allow this to cook undisturbed. Adjust the heat and make it lower as the color of the chicken turns to brown. With the use of a metal spatula, you may turn the chicken pieces every 3 to 4 minutes. Note that the chicken should not necessarily be thoroughly cooked. Well, not yet. Now, put the chicken on a plate and leave the drippings on the pan.

Next, you may add the shallots to the drippings left in the wok. The drippings are more than enough to cook the shallots. Over medium heat, cook the shallot for approximately two to three minutes until they become soft. Until then, you may add the curry powder or curry paste. Cook and stir until your food is fragrant.

The chicken may now be put back on the wok. Stir this well until the chicken is well-combined with the rest of the shallots. You may now put in the coconut milk and the broth. Over high heat, put the mixture to a boil. Once the boiling point is reached, you may add the salt and pepper, bell pepper, and potatoes. Cover the wok and lower the fire to medium. Simmer the mixture for the next fifteen minutes. Now, you may turn the chicken and allow it to brown. The other ingredients have to be closely monitored too.

Wok Recipe #10: Sweet Potato Wok Pudding

The following are the ingredients that you need to prepare: four cups of raw sweet potatoes that have been grated, 1 1/3 cups of milk, 1 cup of sugar, 3 pieces of beaten eggs, ¾ teaspoons of ground all spice, and ¾ teaspoons of ground cinnamon.

To prepare, you need to begin with combining all the ingredients and mixing them thoroughly. Next, you need to pour then into a greased quiche dish. Place the rack in a wok that is filled with water up to 1 inch just below the rack. The water should be brought to boil and the pudding has to be set on the rack.

The wok has to be covered and heat has to be reduced. Simmer the pudding for the next one hour or so. If you wish to add more water, do so only when necessary.

Remove the dish from the wok. Serve this pudding after five minutes, when it is no longer too hot.

Wok Recipe #11: Salmon Smoked in a Wok

This dish will serve two to three people. The following are the ingredients that you need to prepare: ½ cup of soy sauce, ¼ cup of dry sherry or rice wine, 1 tablespoon of ginger root that has been minced, 2 tablespoons of sugar (granulated), 1 pound of salmon fillet, ½ cup of packed brown sugar, 1/3 cup of uncooked rice, ¼ cup of Oolong tea of the traditional

eight minutes until smoke begins to appear. The marinated strips of salmon should be placed on top of the wire rack, with the skin side facing downwards. Now, you may cover the wok and lower the heat to medium. Continue the smoking process until the strips of salmon has developed a very deep and very rich color. Do this for around ten to twelve minutes. For the first ten minutes of smoking, never remove the lid for continuous smoking.

If done properly, the salmon after smoking easily flakes. Turn off the heat and remove the wok and place it somewhere cool. Let the setup stand for the next ten minutes or so. In a bowl, mix together cold water and the cornstarch. Mix until it is smooth. Pour the marinade into the saucepan and heat it using medium fire. Bring the marinade to boil. Add the cornstarch mixture there and stir until the sauce thickens. Serve the salmon with a little sauce. It is best eaten with hot cooked rice and stir-fried veggies.

Wok Recipe #12: Wok-Tossed Eel with glass noodles and turmeric

The following are the ingredients that you need to prepare: 50 grams of bean thread vermicelli, 3 pieces of dried wood type of ear mushrooms, ½ teaspoons of curry powder, ½ teaspoons of turmeric, ½ teaspoons of chili flakes, 2 tablespoons of fish sauce, 1 tablespoon of sugar, 2 tablespoons of vegetable oil, 2 minced garlic cloves, ½ diced onion, ½ wedge sliced onion, 400 grams of eel fillets, deboned and sliced into 3 centimeter pieces, some 45 milliliters of coconut milk, 2 tablespoons of peanuts that have been roasted and crushed, 1 handful of herb for rice paddies sliced roughly, some roughly sliced Coriander leaves, 2 chili pieces diced, and soy sauce for the dip.

First, you need to soak the bean thread glass vermicelli in water for around 20 to 30 minutes. After that, the water has to be drained so that you can cut it into 10 centimeter lengths. Put the mushrooms now in another bowl and soak it for around twenty minutes. Slice thinly and drain.

Next, you may combine the following ingredients in another bowl: turmeric, chili flakes, and curry powder. Set this mixture aside for a while. In a separate bowl, combine sugar, 2 tablespoons of water and fish sauce. Mix very well and set it aside.

You may now heat the wok over medium fire. Add the vegetable oil, diced onion, the garlic, and the lemon grass.

Stir-fry until the mixture is fragrant. Increase heat until the fire is high. Add the eel and for two minutes, stir-fry the eel. Next, you may add the curry powder. Continue stir-frying for the next minute.

By then, you can already add the vermicelli, the ear mushroom, the onion wedges, and the mixture with the fish sauce. Toss the ingredients really well and pour in the coconut milk. Continue stir frying for the next two minutes.

Finally, garnish with crushed roasted peanuts, coriander, and the rice paddy herbs. This meal is best served hot with cooked rice, and dipping.

Wok Recipe #13: The Real Chinese Fried Rice cooked in a Wok

Note that this recipe serves five to six people. The following are the ingredients that you have to prepare: four cups of rice (the jasmine variety), some wok oil, two to three dashes of ginger that has been grated, 1 whole onion chopped, ¾ cup of chicken stock, 1 ½ teaspoon of sugar, 1 teaspoon of sesame oil, 3 pieces of scrambled eggs, 1 cup of frozen carrot and peas, 2 to three teaspoons of salt, and some soy sauce according to taste.

Get 4 cups of cooked jasmine rice. Set this aside in a cool place or in a refrigerator. Next, you may scramble the eggs in a different pan. Do your best to fold the eggs so that they can be cut into strips.

Heat the wok. Add three to four tablespoons of vegetable oil. Use medium heat only. Now, you may sauté the onion until it is transparent for three minutes or so. Then you can add the frozen carrots and peas followed by soy sauce.

Now, you may add the rice. Make sure that you separate the grains with the use of your fingers. Mix the rice well with the veggies. Add some more vegetable oil and sesame seed oil. Put the ginger, chicken stock, and sugar. Top with the strips of scrambled egg.

Put the heat to high and add preferred amount of soy sauce. Stir-fry until desired consistency is achieved. Do your best to do this using the highest heat level.

Stir-fry until all the liquids evaporated. Add little amount of salt to taste. Serve while hot.

Chapter 3 – Asian Soup Recipes

Wok Recipe #1: Prawn Laksa

This meal will serve two to three people. The following are the ingredients that you need to prepare: 3 fried tofu puffs cut into julienned strips, 1/2 tablespoon seeds of cumin, 1 teaspoon chopped fresh ginger, 1 chopped onion, 1/2 teaspoon ground turmeric, 2 cloves garlic, 1 1/2 stems sliced white part of lemon grass, 3/4 tablespoon coriander seeds, 3 roughly chopped macadamia nuts, 3 roughly chopped small fresh red chilies, 1 1/2 teaspoons shrimp paste, 1/2 quart chicken stock, 1/8 cup vegetable oil, 1 1/2 cups coconut milk, 1 1/4 tablespoons lime juice, 2 fresh kaffir lime leaves, 1 tablespoon grated palm sugar, 1 tablespoon fish sauce, 3/4 lbs raw medium prawns peeled and deveined with tails intact, 4 ounces rice pasta or vermicelli (dried), 1/2 cup tailed bean sprouts, 1 1/2 tablespoons fresh mint chopped, 1/3 cup fresh coriander leaves, lime or lemon wedges

First, place a small skillet over medium heat and dry fry the coriander seeds for about a minute, tossing frequently. Grind to a fine consistency. Do the same thing to the cumin seeds.

Next, combine the ground coriander and cumin with the onion, turmeric, ginger, lemon grass, garlic, macadamia nuts, shrimp paste, and chili in a blender or food processor. Pour in 1/4 cup of chicken stock and process until you get a paste.

Place the wok on low heat and grease with the oil. Sauté the paste for about 2 minutes in the wok, then add the rest of the stock and bring to a boil. Lower the heat and let simmer for about 12 minutes to thicken. Stir in the coconut milk, lime leaves, sugar, lime juice, and fish sauce. Let simmer for about 3 minutes. Put the prawns into the mixture and let simmer for about 2 minutes or until well done and pink. Do not cover and do not let it boil.

Soak the vermicelli for 6 minutes in boiling water, or until tender. Drain and put into serving bowls and add some bean sprouts. Pour the soup on top and add the tofu, bean sprouts, coriander, and mint. Garnish with lime wedges and serve.

Wok Recipe #2: Spicy Vietnamese Beef and Pork Noodle Soup

This meal will serve two people. The following are the ingredients that you need to prepare: 5 ounces beef fillet steak, 1/8 cup vegetable oil, 5 ounces pork leg fillet cut into 1 1/4 inch cubes, 1 small onion cut into thin wedges, 1 quart beef stock, 1 lemon grass stem, 1 tablespoon fish sauce, 1/2 teaspoon ground dried shrimp, 1/2 teaspoon sugar, 1 sliced large fresh red chili, 6 1/2 ounces fresh round rice noodles, 1 cup tailed bean sprouts, 1/4 cup fresh mint, 1/4 cup fresh coriander leaves, thinly sliced fresh chili (optional), lemon wedges

First, put the beef in the freezer for half an hour, then slice across the grain into paper thin pieces. Set aside.

Place the wok over medium high heat and grease with a tablespoon of oil. Reduce to medium heat and cook stir fry the pork for 2 minutes or until browned. Remove from the wok and set aside.

Grease the wok with another tablespoon of oil and stir fry the onion until soft, about 2 minutes. Add the stock and a cup of water. Crush half of the lemon grass stem and add it to the wok. Put the pork back into the wok and bring to a boil, then lower the heat and let simmer for 15 minutes or until the pork becomes tender. Remove any fat that gets to the surface. Thinly slice the other half of the lemon grass stem. Take out the crushed lemon grass stem from the broth and add the fish sauce, dried shrimp, and sugar. Stir and let simmer.

Place a small skillet over medium flame and pour in the rest of the oil. Let it heat up then cook the sliced lemon grass and chili in it for about 2 minutes. Scrape this into the broth and stir. Let simmer.

Put the rice noodles into a heatproof bowl and pour boiling water on top until completely covered. Separate the noodles, then drain and rinse. Divide them among four soup bowls.

Bring the broth to a boil, and then reduce heat. Put the bean sprouts into the broth and add the beef fillet steak. The heat from the soup will cook the beef to a medium rare. Divide the soup between the bowls and sprinkle mint, coriander, and fresh chili on top. Serve immediately with lemon wedges.

Wok Recipe #3: Japanese Vegetable Ramen Noodle Soup

This meal will serve three people. The following are the ingredients that you need to prepare: 4 ounces fresh ramen noodles, 1/2 tablespoon vegetable oil, 1/2 tablespoon finely chopped fresh ginger, 1 crushed garlic clove, 2 1/2 ounces oyster mushrooms sliced in half, 1/2 thinly sliced small zucchini, 1 leek cut in half lengthwise and thinly sliced, 2 ounces snow peas cut in half diagonally, 2 ounces fried tofu puffs cut into julienne strips, 1/6 cup white miso paste, 1/6 cup light soy sauce, 1/8 cup mirin

Fill a large saucepan with salted water and bring to a boil over medium high heat. Put the noodles into the saucepan and cook for 2 minutes, stirring frequently to prevent clumping. Drain and rinse under cold running water, then drain thoroughly.

Place a wok over medium heat and grease with the vegetable oil. Stir fry the garlic and ginger for 30 seconds, then add the zucchini, oyster mushrooms, leek, snow peas, and sliced tofu puffs. Stir fry for 3 minutes.

Add about 3/4 quart of water and bring to a boil, then lower the heat and let simmer. Add the miso paste, mirin, and soy sauce and stir to combine. Do not bring to a boil. Add the bean sprouts and sesame oil and stir.

Put the noodles into the soup bowls and ladle the soup on top. Top with sliced spring onions and enoki mushrooms, then serve.

Wok Recipe #4: Eight Treasure Soup

This meal will serve three people. The following are the ingredients that you need to prepare: 2 dried shiitake mushrooms, 1/2 tablespoon vegetable oil, 1/2 teaspoon sesame oil, 1 teaspoon finely chopped fresh ginger, 1/2 tablespoon finely chopped spring onion, 1 ounce Chinese ham or bacon cut into thin strips, 1/2 quart chicken stock, 1/2 tablespoon rice wine, 1/2 tablespoon soy sauce, 4 ounces chicken breast fillet, 1/2 carrot cut into 1/2 inch slices, 6 small raw prawns peeled and deveined, 3 1/4 ounces firm tofu cut into 3/4 inch cubes, 25 grams sliced bamboo shoots, 50 grams chopped English spinach, 1 spring onion thinly sliced diagonally

Make sure to soak the mushrooms in 1/4 cup boiling water for 20 minutes first. After that, squeeze them dry and set aside the soaking liquid. Chop off and throw away the woody stalks. Cut the caps into quarters.

Place the wok over high heat and heat through. Pour in the oils to coat the wok. Sauté the ginger, spring onion and bacon for 10 seconds, then pour in the stock, rice wine, soy sauce, mushroom soaking liquid, and 1/4 teaspoon salt. Bring to a boil, then put the chicken into the mixture. Lower the heat and put it on low, then put the lid on the wok. Poach the chicken for about half an hour, then remove the chicken from the stock using a slotted spoon. Set aside to cool, then shred the chicken.

Bring the stock to a boil then add the carrot. Cook for 5 minutes, then add the tofu, prawns, bamboo shoots, shredded chicken, and spinach. Reduce heat to low and cook for 5 minutes, then serve.

Wok Recipe #5: Hot and Sour Prawn Soup

This meal will serve one to two people. The following are the ingredients that you need to prepare: 1 lb raw medium prawns, 1 tablespoon vegetable oil, 1 stem white part of lemon grass, 1 tablespoon tom yam paste, 2 fresh kaffir lime leaves, 1 1/2 thinly sliced small red chilies, 1/4 cup fish sauce, 1/4 cup lime juice, 1 teaspoon grated palm sugar, 2 tablespoons fresh coriander leaves, 2 thinly sliced spring onion

Peel and devein the raw prawns first, but make sure to keep the tails intact. Set aside the shells and heads. Store the prawns in a covered container in the refrigerator.

Place a wok over medium heat and grease it with the oil. Cook the prawn heads and shells for about 7 minutes, or until they become orange.

Add the tom yam paste and 1/8 cup of water. Cook for about a minute, then add 1 1/4 quart water. Bring to a boil, then lower the heat and let simmer for about 20 minutes. Pour through a strainer, and pour the stock back into the wok.

Put the prawns, into the wok. Bruise the lemon grass and add it to the wok, along with the chili and lime leaves. Let simmer for about 5 minutes, or until the prawns are cooked through. Add the fish sauce, sugar, lime juice, coriander, and spring onion. Stir well, then remove the lemon grass and serve immediately.

Wok Recipe #6: Scallops with Soba Noodles and Dashi Broth

This meal will serve one to two people. The following are the ingredients that you need to prepare: 4 ounces dried soba noodles, 1/8 cup mirin, 1/8 cup light soy sauce, 1 teaspoon dashi granules, 1 teaspoon rice vinegar, 1 diagonally sliced spring onion, 1/2 teaspoon finely chopped fresh ginger, 12 large scallops (no roe), 3 chopped fresh black fungus (or used dried, but make sure to soak it in warm water for at least 20 minutes), shredded 1/2 sheet nori

First, boil some water in a saucepan and add the noodles. Separate them with a fork, then bring to a boil. Add half a cup of cold water and bring to a boil; do this thrice. Drain the noodles, then rinse under cold water.

Combine the soy sauce, mirin, vinegar, 1 3/4 cups water, and dashi in a non-stick wok. Place over medium heat and ring to a boil, then lower the heat and let simmer for 3 minutes. Add the ginger and spring onion and let simmer.

Preheat a hot plate or chargrill pan o high heat, then sear the scallops for half a minute per side. Set aside.

Put the noodles and black fungus into two large deep serving bowls, then ladle the broth into each. Add 6 scallops on top of each bowl, then top with shredded nori and serve.

Wok Recipe #7: Chicken Noodle Soup

This meal will serve two people. The following are the ingredients that you need to prepare: 1 1/2 ounces fresh egg noodles, 3/4 quart chicken stock, 1 tablespoon soy sauce, 1/2 tablespoon mirin, 1 inch piece fresh ginger root cut into julienne strips, 1 thinly sliced chicken breast fillet, 1 lb baby bok choy with stalks trimmed and leaves separated, fresh coriander leaves, sweet chili sauce

Place a saucepan filled with water over medium flame and add the noodles. Cook for a minute, then drain and rinse.

Put the stock into the wok and place the wok over medium flame. Bring to a simmer and then stir in the soy sauce, ginger, mirin, chicken, and cooked noodles. Cook for about 5 minutes or until the chicken becomes tender and the noodles are warmed. Skim off any fats that come to the surface.

Add the bok choy and cook for an additional 2 minutes or until the bok choy becomes wilted. Divide between two deep soup bowls and top with coriander. Serve with sweet chili sauce, if preferred.

Wok Recipe #8: Pork and Buttered Corn Ramen Noodle Soup

This meal will serve one to two people. The following are the ingredients that you need to prepare: 3 1/4 ounces (1 piece) Chinese barbecued pork fillet, 1 small fresh corn cob, 1 teaspoon peanut oil, 3 1/4 ounces dried ramen noodles, 1/2 teaspoon grated fresh ginger, 1 tablespoon mirin, 3/4 liter chicken stock, 1 tablespoon mirin, 1 spring onion sliced diagonally, 2 teaspoons unsalted butter, 1/2 spring onion sliced diagonally

Slice the pork thinly. Remove the kernels from the corn cob by holding the corn cob up and slicing it down the sides using a very sharp knife.

Fill a saucepan with some water and bring it to a boil. Cook the ramen noodles for 4 minutes in the boiling water, or until tender. Drain, rinse in cold water, and drain once more.

Place a wok over high heat and grease with oil. Stir fry the ginger for about a minute, then add the stock, 1 cup of water, and mirin. Bring everything to a boil, then lower the heat and let simmer for 6 minutes.

Put the pork in the broth and cook for 5 minutes. Put the spring onion and corn kernels into the broth and cook for an additional 4 minutes, or until kernels become tender.

Separate the noodles under hot water, then divide the noodles into mounds between two deep bowls. Ladle the liquid over the noodles and arrange the corn and pork on top. Add a teaspoon of unsalted butter over each mound and garnish with spring onion. Serve instantly.

Wok Recipe #9: Beef Pho

This meal will serve two people. The following are the ingredients that you need to prepare: 1/2 quart, beef stock, 1 star anise, 1 inch piece fresh ginger, 1 pigs' trotters sliced in half, 1/4 onion studded with 1 clove, 1 stem lemon grass, 1 crushed garlic clove, 1/8 teaspoon ground white pepper, 1/2 tablespoon fish sauce, 3 1/4 ounces fresh thin round rice noodles, 5 ounces thinly sliced beef fillet, 1/2 cup tailed bean sprouts, 1 thinly sliced spring onion, 1/4 cup chopped fresh coriander leaves,2 tablespoons chopped fresh Vietnamese mint, 1/2 fresh red chili sliced thinly, 1 lime sliced into quarters

Place a wok over medium flame and combine the beef stock, star anise, pigs' trotters, ginger, lemon grass, onion, white pepper, and garlic in it. Bring to a boil, then lower the heat and and let simmer. Cover and cook for 20 minutes. Strain the soup, then put the stock back into the wok and add the fish sauce. Stir to combine.

Place the noodles inside a heatproof bowl and pour boiling water to cover. Carefully separate the noodles using a fork. Drain thoroughly and rinse gently under cold running water.

Place the noodles into two deep soup bowls and add the beef strips on top then ladle the soup into the bowls. Place the mint, lime quarters, coriander, chili, and fish sauce in small serving bowls for the diners to take from each as they eat.

Wok Recipe #10: Thai Chicken and Galangal Soup

This meal will serve two people. The following are the ingredients that you need to prepare: 1 inch piece fresh galangal cut into thin slices, 1 cup coconut milk, 1/2 cup chicken stock, 2 fresh kaffir lime leaves, torn, 1/2 tablespoon well rinsed finely chopped fresh coriander roots, 1/2 lb chicken breast fillet, cut into thin strips, 1 teaspoon finely chopped fresh red chilies, 1 tablespoon fish sauce, 3/4 tablespoon lime juice, 1 1/2 teaspoon grated palm sugar, 2 tablespoons fresh coriander leaves

Put the coconut milk, galangal, stock, coriander root, and lime leaves in the wok. Place the wok over medium high heat and bring to a boil, then let simmer for about 10 minutes, stirring every now and then.

put the chicken and chili into the wok and let simmer for 8 minutes, or until the chicken is well done. Add the fish sauce, palm sugar, and lime juice and stir to combine. Cook for 1 minute, then add the coriander leaves. Stir to mix and serve immediately.

Chapter 4 – Deep Fried Recipes

Wok Recipe #1: Lemon Chicken

This meal will serve two people. The following are the ingredients that you need to prepare: 1/2 lb trimmed chicken fillets, 1/2 lightly beaten egg, 1/4 cup lemon juice, 1/2 tablespoon white vinegar, 1/8 cup sugar, 3/4 tablespoons cornflour plus more to coat, sliced spring onion, lemon, salt, freshly ground black pepper, oil for deep frying

First, season the chicken fillet using salt and freshly ground black pepper. Dip the pieces in the egg, then dip it in a bowl of cornflour. Shake off and set aside.

Pour oil into the wok until it is about a third full. Heat to 350 degrees F. You can also test its heat by placing a cub of bread in it; if it turns brown in 15 seconds, it is ready. Cook the chicken for 6 minutes, turning occasionally, or until golden brown and well done. Place on paper towels to drain.

In a saucepan over low heat, stir together the lemon juice, sugar, vinegar, and 1/8 cup of water. Bring to a boil as you stir, then lower the heat and let simmer for 1 minute. Combine the 3/4 tablespoon cornflour and 1/8 cup water. Stir this into the saucepan mixture very well until thickened.

Slice the chicken fillets and arrange them on a serving plate. Pour t he sauce on top and garnish with lemon and spring onion.

Wok Recipe #2: Spiced Prawn Pakoras

This meal will serve two to three people. The following are the ingredients that you need to prepare: 1/3 cup chickpea flour, 1/4 teaspoon baking powder, 1/2 teaspoon ground coriander, 1/8 teaspoon ground turmeric, 1/4 teaspoon ground cumin, 1/4 teaspoon chili powder, 1/2 tablespoon egg white, 8 raw medium prawns peeled and deveined but with tails intact, oil for deep frying, 1/2 cup plain yogurt, 1 1/2 tablespoons chopped fresh coriander leaves, 1/2 teaspoon ground cumin, garam masala

Sift together the baking powder, turmeric, coriander, cumin, baking powder, besan, and chili powder into a bowl. Season with a bit of salt, then form a pit in the center. Pour 1/2 cup of water into the pit as you stir to mix.

Pour oil into the wok until it is about a third full. Heat to 315 degrees F. You can also test its heat by placing a cub of bread in it; if it turns brown in 30 seconds, it is ready.

Whisk the egg white until it can form soft peaks, then fold it into the mixture. Dip the prawns into the mixture by holding onto the tail, then put it into the hot wok and cook for 2 minutes or until pale golden. Place on paper towels to drain.

Make the dipping sauce by mixing together the yogurt, cumin, and coriander. Top with garam masala and serve with the spiced prawns.

Wok Recipe #3: Vegetable Pakoras

This meal will serve two people. The following are the ingredients that you need to prepare: 1/6 cup chickpea flour, 1/6 cup self raising flour, 1/6 cup soy flour, 1/4 teaspoon ground turmeric, 1/4 teaspoon ground coriander, 1/2 teaspoon cayenne pepper, 1/2 small fresh green chili seeded and chopped finely, 3 1/4 ounces cauliflower, 2 1/4 ounces orange sweet potato, 3 ounces eggplant, 3 ounces fresh asparagus, oil for deep frying

Sift together the besan, soy flour and self raising flour into a bowl. Stir in the cayenne pepper, turmeric, chili, ground coriander, and 1/2 teaspoon of salt. Gradually stir in 1/2 cup of cold water until you get a batter. Set aside for 15 minutes.

Preheat the oven to 250 degrees F or to very low heat.

Slice the cauliflower into florets and slice the orange sweet potato and eggplant into 1/4 inch pieces. Slice the asparagus into 2 1/2 inch pieces.

Pour oil into the wok until it is about a third full. Heat to 325 degrees F. You can also test its heat by placing a cub of bread in it; if it turns brown in 20 seconds, it is ready.

Dip the pieces of vegetable into the batter then place them into the hot wok and cook for 1 minute or until light golden. Use a slotted spoon to remove them from the wok and place them on paper towels to drain. Place them in the preheated oven to keep warm, then serve, preferably with plain yogurt.

Wok Recipe #4: Nori Wrapped Fried Mushrooms

This meal will serve two people. The following are the ingredients that you need to prepare: 1/6 cup Japanese soy sauce, 1 teaspoon grated fresh ginger, 1 3/4 ounces mirin, 1 teaspoon sugar, 1 1/2 toasted nori sheets, 6 open cup mushrooms with stalks removed, 6 1/2 ounces chilled soda water, 1/2 lightly beaten egg, 1/2 cup tempura flour, 1 tablespoon wasabi powder

Make the sauce by combining the mirin, sugar, soy sauce, ginger, and 1/2 tablespoon of water into a saucepan. Place over medium heat and stir until the sugar is dissolved. Cover and set aside.

Snip the nori sheets into six pieces of 1 1/2 inch wide strips using scissors. Wrap each mushroom with a strip and wet the end of each nori strip to stick the ends together. With a vegetable peeler, slice the orange sweet potato into ribbon strips.

Pour oil into the wok until it is about a third full. Heat to 375 degrees F. You can also test its heat by placing a cub of bread in it; if it turns brown in 10 seconds, it is ready. Cook the sweet potato for 30 seconds or until crisp and golden. Drain on paper towels and season, then keep warm.

Beat together the egg and the soda water. Gradually stir in the tempura flour and wasabi powder. Make sure that the batter is still lumpy. Dip the mushrooms in the batter and cook for 1 minute in the wok, turning only once, until crisp and golden. Drain on paper towels and season with a bit of salt. Serve with the sauce and crisp sweet potato ribbons.

Wok Recipe #5: Salt and Pepper Tofu Puffs

This meal will serve two to three people. The following are the ingredients that you need to prepare: 1/4 cup sweet chili sauce, 1 cup cornflour, 1 tablespoon lemon juice, 1/2 tablespoon ground white pepper ,1 teaspoon caster sugar, 1 cup cornflour, 1 tablespoon salt, 6 ounces fried tofu puffs cut int half and patted dry, 2 lightly beaten egg whites, peanut oil for deep frying, lemon wedges

In a bowl, mix together the lemon juice and chili sauce. Set aside. In another bowl, mix together the salt, pepper, cornflour, and caster sugar. First dip each tofu puff in the egg white, then toss each piece in the salt and pepper mixture.

Pour oil into the wok until it is about a third full. Heat to 350 degrees F. You can also test its heat by placing a cub of bread in it; if it turns brown in 15 seconds, it is ready. Cook each coated tofu puff for 1 minute or until crisp, then drain on paper towels. Serve immediately with the chili sauce and lemon wedges.

Wok Recipe #6: Thai Stuffed Chicken Wings

This meal will serve three people. The following are the ingredients that you need to prepare: 6 large chicken wings, 1/2 tablespoon grated palm sugar, 1/3 ounce dried rice vermicelli, 1 tablespoon fish sauce, 3 1/4 ounces pork mince, 2 chopped cloves garlic, 1 chopped spring onion, 1/2 chopped small fresh red chili, 1 1/2 tablespoons chopped fresh coriander leaves, peanut oil for deep frying, well seasoned rice flour to coat, sweet chili sauce

With a very sharp knife, scrape down each chicken wing to the bone and push the meat and skin from the fattest end to the connecting joint. Twist and pull the bone from the socket and throw it away or set it aside to make stock.

In a bowl of boiling water, soak the vermicelli for 6 minutes, then drain thoroughly. Cut them into 3/4 inch pieces using scissors, then set aside.

In a bowl, mix together the fish sauce and palm sugar until the sugar is dissolved. Transfer into a food processor and add the pork mince , garlic, chili, and spring onion into the mixture. Process until thoroughly combined, then scrape into a bowl and add the noodles and coriander.

Form the mixture into 6 balls and stuff each ball into the boned out piece of chicken wing. Seal the openings using a toothpick. Arrange the chicken wings in a metal steamer and place over a wok filled with simmering water. Make sure that the water does not touch the base of the steamer. Cover and steam for 6 minutes, the take the wings out and set aside to firm.

Pour oil into the wok until it is about a third full. Heat to 400 degrees F. You can also test its heat by placing a cub of bread in it; if it turns brown in 5 seconds, it is ready. Coat the wings in the seasoned rice flour and deep fry for 3 minutes, or until golden brown. Drain the chicken wings on paper towels, take out the toothpicks, and serve with sweet chili sauce.

Wok Recipe #7: Thai Fish Cakes with Dipping Sauce

This meal will serve three people. The following are the ingredients that you need to prepare: 1/4 cup sugar, 1/8 cup white vinegar, 1/2 small fresh red chili chopped, 1/2 tablespoon fish sauce, 1/4 cup finely chopped carrot, 1/4 cup peeled, seeded, and finely chopped cucumber, 1/2 tablespoon chopped roasted peanuts, 1/2 lb red fish fillets skin removed, 3/4 tablespoon Thai red curry paste, 1/8 cup fish sauce, 1/8 cup sugar, 1/2 beaten egg, 3 1/4 ounces sliced snake beans, 5 finely chopped fresh lime leaves, oil for deep frying

Make the dipping sauce first by combining the vinegar, sugar, fish sauce, and chili along with 1/4 cup water in a saucepan. Place over medium flame and let simmer for 5 minutes, or until it becomes a bit thickened. Set aside to cool, then add the carrot, cucumber, and roasted peanuts. Set aside.

Place the fish into a food processor and blend to a smooth consistency. Put the sugar, fish sauce, curry paste, and egg in, then process until thoroughly combined. Add the beans and lime leaves, then mold into balls the size of golf balls. Flatten them down to create patties.

Place the wok on the stovetop and fill it to about a third full of the cooking oil. Heat to 350 degrees F. You can also test its heat by placing a cub of bread in it; if it turns brown in 15 seconds, it is ready. Cook the fish cakes for 3 minutes, turning a few times. Drain thoroughly on paper towels and serve with the dipping sauce.

Wok Recipe #8: Bondas

This meal will serve two to three people. The following are the ingredients that you need to prepare: 1 teaspoon vegetable oil, 1/2 teaspoon brown mustard seeds, 1/2 finely chopped onion, 1 teaspoon freshly grated ginger, 2 curry leaves, 1 1/2 small green chilies chopped finely, 1 lb and 3 1/4 ounces potatoes diced and cooked with a dash of ground turmeric, 1 tablespoon lemon juice, 1/6 cup chopped fresh coriander leaves, oil for deep frying, 1/2 cup chickpea flour, 1/8 cup self raising flour, 1/8 cup rice flour, 1/8 teaspoon ground turmeric, 1/2 teaspoon chili powder

First, place the wok over medium heat and grease it with oil. Saute the mustard seeds for half a minute, then add the ginger, onion, chili, and curry leaves. Cook for about a minute, then add the turmeric, potato, and a teaspoon of water. Stir for 2 minutes, then remove from heat and set aside to cool.

Add the coriander leaves and lemon juice to the mustard seed mixture and season to taste. Form the mixture into 12 balls.

In a bowl, sift together the turmeric, chili powder, 1/8 teaspoon of salt, and the flours. Create a pit in the center and slowly beat in 2/3 cup of water to create a smooth batter.

Place the wok on the stovetop and fill it to about a third full of the cooking oil. Heat to 350 degrees F. You can also test its heat by placing a cub of bread in it; if it turns brown in 15 seconds, it is ready. Dip each ball into the smooth batter, then deep fry in the hot wok for 1 minute, or until golden.

Drain on paper towels and season with salt. Serve immediately.

Chapter 5 – Steamed Recipes

Wok Recipe #1: Steamed Fish

This meal will serve two to three people. The following are the ingredients that you need to prepare: 1/8 cup white miso paste, 1/2 tablespoon vegetable oil, 1 crushed garlic clove, 3/4 tablespoon grated fresh ginger, 1 tablespoon light soy sauce, 1 tablespoon oyster sauce, 1 1/2 lbs whole red snapper scaled and cleaned, 2 spring onions sliced, fresh coriander leaves

In a food processor, blend together the oil, garlic, miso paste, soy sauce, ginger, and oyster sauce to a smooth paste.

Create four deep diagonal slashes on either side of the fish. If the fish cannot fit inside the steamer, remove the head. Rub half of the paste on one side of the fish. Flip and repeat on the other side.

Put the fish on a plate and cover using plastic wrap. Marinate in the refrigerator for 3 hours or more.

Line a bamboo steamer using a baking sheet. Put the fish into the steamer and top with spring onion. Cover and steam on top of a wok with simmering water for 20 minutes or until the fish is well done. Refill the boiling water, if needed.

Take the fish out of the steamer and spoon the juices on top. Garnish with coriander and serve with vegetables and rice.

Wok Recipe #2: Steamed Mussels with Lemon Grass and Ginger

This meal will serve two to three people. The following are the ingredients that you need to prepare: 2 lbs black mussels, 1/2 tablespoon fish sauce, 1 crushed garlic clove, 2 small red Asian shallots sliced thinly, 1/2 tablespoon finely shredded fresh ginger, 1 bird's eye chili seeded and sliced thinly, 1 bruised white part stem lemon grass, 2 fresh kaffir lime leaves, 1/2 tablespoon lime juice, 1/2 lime sliced into wedges

First, scrub the mussels thoroughly using a stiff brush. Take out the hairy beards and throw away any broken or open mussels. Rinse thoroughly.

Combine the fish sauce and 1/4 cup water in a wok and place over medium high heat. Bring to a boil, then add mussels in it. Add the garlic, shallots, chili, ginger, lime leaves, and lemon grass. Cover and steam for 2 minutes, shaking the wok throughout, until the mussels become opened. Take out the mussels using a slotted spoon and throw away any that have not opened. Put the mussels into a large serving bowl.

Put the lime juice into the wok with the cooking liquid. Season to taste with salt and pepper, then pour the mixture on top of the mussels and serve with lime wedges.

Wok Recipe #3: Gyoza

This meal will serve two to three people. The following are the ingredients that you need to prepare: 2 1/2 ounces very finely shredded Chinese cabbage, 3 1/2 ounces pork mince, 1 finely chopped garlic clove, 1 teaspoon finely chopped fresh ginger, 1 teaspoon cornflour, 1 finely chopped spring onion, 1/2 tablespoon light soy sauce, 1 teaspoon Chinese rice wine, 20 round Shanghai dumpling wrappers, 1 teaspoon sesame oil, 1 tablespoon vegetable oil, 1/4 cup chicken stock

Place the cabbage and 1/4 teaspoon of salt in a colander. Toss to season, then set aside for half an hour, stirring occasionally.

In a mixing bowl, combine the pork mince, ginger, cornflour, spring onion, garlic, rice wine, sesame oil, and soy sauce using your hands.

Rinse the cabbage under cold running water and press dry using paper towels. Add the cabbage to the pork mince mixture and mix well.

Put a teaspoon of the mixture in the center of each Shanghai dumpling wrapper and brush the inside edge of each with a bit of water. Press the two edges together to create a half circle, then pleat the edges firmly to seal.

Heat 1/2 teaspoon of vegetable oil in the wok over medium high heat and cook the gyozas for 2 minutes with the flat side down. Lower the heat and add half of the stock. Cover and steam for 3 minutes, or until the stock has evaporated. Remove the gyozas and keep warm. Do the same for the second batch of gyozas.

Serve the gyozas with Chinese black vinegar or soy sauce.

Wok Recipe #4: Pork and Chive Dumplings

This meal will serve two to three people. The following are the ingredients that you need to prepare: 1/2 teaspoon vegetable oil, 1 crushed garlic clove, 1 teaspoon finely grated fresh ginger, 4 ounces garlic chives sliced into 1/2 inch lengths, 3 1/4 ounces pork mince, 1 tablespoon oyster sauce, 1 1/2 teaspoons Chinese rice wine, 1 teaspoon light soy sauce, 1/4 teaspoon sesame oil, 1/2 teaspoon cornflour, 12 row gow gee wrappers

Put the wok over high heat and heat the vegetable oil. Stir fry the ginger, garlic, and garlic fries for 1 minute, then remove from heat and set aside.

In a non-metallic bowl, mix together the oyster sauce, soy sauce, rice wine, cornflour, sesame oil, and pork mince. Cover with plastic wrap and refrigerate for approximately 3 hours to marinate. Once the vegetable mixture has cooled, add it to the pork mince mixture and refrigerate for an additional 3 hours.

Place 2 teaspoons of the mixture in the center of each gow gee wrapper and brush the inside edge of each with a bit of water. Fold the sides together to create a semicircle, then pinch to seal.

Line a double bamboo steamer with baking sheets and arrange the dumplings in a single layer in the steamer baskets. Cover and steam for 12 minutes on top of a wok with simmering water. Serve immediately.

Wok Recipe 5: Steamed Vegetable Rolls

This meal will serve two to three people. The following are the ingredients that you need to prepare: 1/8 cup hot chili sauce, 1 tablespoon hoisin sauce, 1/2 tablespoon crushed unsalted peanuts, 1/2 tablespoon light soy sauce, 1/3 ounce dried shiitake mushrooms, 4 ounces shredded Chinese cabbage, 1 small carrot grated, 2 sliced spring onions, 1/8 cup julienned bamboo shoots, 1 crushed garlic clove, 1 tablespoon finely chopped water chestnuts, 1 tablespoon chopped fresh coriander leaves, 3/4 tablespoon fish sauce ,1/2 teaspoon grated fresh ginger, 1/2 tablespoon soy sauce, 1 bean curd sheet

Make the dipping sauce first by mixing together the hot chili sauce, light soy sauce, hoisin sauce, and crushed peanuts in a bowl. Set aside.

Soak the shiitake mushrooms in hot water for 20 minutes. Drain and chop off the stalks. Finely shred the caps and squeeze out excess water. Mix together the caps with the shredded Chinese cabbage, carrot, onion, bamboo shoots, garlic, water chestnuts, coriander, fish sauce, soy sauce, and fresh ginger.

If the bean curd sheet is big, cut it up into the proper size. Soak the bean curd sheet in warm water for half a minute, then take it out of the water and squeeze it out carefully. Spread it out and spoon the mixture into it. Roll it up to form a log, tucking the insides.

Line a bamboo steamer with baking paper and put the rolls with the seam sides down in a single layer. Cover and steam for 20 minutes on top of a wok with simmering water. Take the steamer off the heat and set aside to cook. Once firm, slice the log into bite sized pieces and serve with the dipping sauce.

Chapter 6 – Stir Fry Recipes

Wok Recipe #1: Chili Beef

This meal will serve two to three people. The following are the ingredients that you need to prepare: 1/8 cup kecap manis, 1 1/4 teaspoons sambal oelek, 1 crushed garlic clove, 1/2 tablespoon grated palm sugar, 1/4 teaspoon ground coriander, 1/2 teaspoon sesame oil, 7 1/2 ounces lean beef fillet sliced thinly across the grain, 1/2 tablespoon peanut oil, 1 tablespoon chopped roasted peanuts, 1 1/2 tablespoons chopped fresh coriander leaves

First, mix together the kecap manis, garlic, sambal oelek, palm sugar, coriander, 1 tablespoon of water, and sesame oil in a mixing bowl. Add the beef and toss to coat. Cover the bowl with plastic wrap and refrigerate for at least 20 minutes.

Place a wok over high heat and heat the peanut oil. Stir fry the beef for 3 minutes, or until browned. Serve on a platter and top with fresh coriander and chopped peanuts.

Wok Recipe #2: Yakisoba

This meal will serve two to three people. The following are the ingredients that you need to prepare: 2 dried shiitake mushrooms, 1 1/2 teaspoons finely chopped fresh ginger, 3/4 lbs Hokkien noodles, 1 finely chopped large garlic clove, 5 ounces lean beef fillet sliced thinly across the grain, 3 rashers streaky bacon cut into 1 1/4 inch pieces, 1 tablespoon peanut oil, 1/4 teaspoon sesame oil, 3 thin spring onions sliced into 1 1/4 inch lengths, 1/2 small green pepper sliced thinly, 1/2 carrot sliced thinly on the diagonal, 3 1/2 ounces shredded Chinese cabbage, shredded nori and pickled ginger, 1/8 cup Japanese soy sauce, 1 tablespoon Worcestershire sauce, 3/4 tablespoon Japanese rice vinegar, 1/2 tablespoon sake, 1/2 tablespoon tomato sauce, 1/2 tablespoon mirin, 1/2 tablespoon oyster sauce, 1 teaspoon soft brown sugar

Soak the shiitake mushrooms in boiling water for 20 minutes, then squeeze dry and set aside a tablespoon of the liquid. Chop off the stalks and slice the caps thinly.

Place the noodles in a heatproof bowl and pour boiling water on them until covered. Soak for 1 minute, then drain and separate.

Mix together half the ginger and garlic in a bowl, then add the beef. Set aside to marinate.

Create the sauce by combining the tablespoon of mushroom liquid with the remaining ginger and garlic, Japanese soy sauce, Worcestershire sauce, rice vinegar, mirin, sake, tomato and oyster sauces, and soft brown sugar.

Place the wok over medium high heat and cook the bacon for 2 minutes. Transfer to a bowl. Mix together the peanut oil and sesame oil. Set the heat on high and add a bit of the oil mixture. Stir fry the beef for 40 seconds, then add the bacon. Add more of the oil mixture and stir fry the spring onion, pepper, and carrot with the meat for 1 minute. Add the Chinese cabbage and mushrooms and stir fry for 30 seconds. Transfer the mixture into a bowl.

Pour the rest of the oil mixture into the wok and stir fry the noodles for 1 minute. Put the meat mixture back into the wok and pour the sauce on top. Stir fry for 2 minutes. Serve the noodles in deep bowls and top with shredded nori and pickled ginger.

Wok Recipe #3: Satay Chicken Stir Fry

This meal will serve two to three people. The following are the ingredients that you need to prepare: 3/4 tablespoon peanut oil, 3 spring onions cut into 1 1/4 inch pieces, 1/2 lb and 5 ounces chicken breast fillets sliced thinly on the diagonal, 3/4 tablespoon Thai red curry paste, 1/6 cup crunchy peanut butter, 4 1/4 ounces coconut milk, 1 teaspoon soft brown sugar, 3/4 tablespoon lime juice

First,place the wok over high heat. Heat half of the peanut oil and stir fry the spring onion until lightly soft. Remove and set aside.

Heat more peanut oil in the wok and stir fry the chicken for 1 minute, then remove from the wok.

Add more oil and stir fry the curry paste. Add the coconut milk, sugar, peanut butter, and 1/2 cup water. Stir fry and bring to a boil for 3 minutes, or until thickened.

Put the spring onion and chicken back into the wok and stir fry for 2 minutes. Add the lime juice, season with salt and pepper if needed, stir to mix, and serve.

Wok Recipe #4: Pork with Plum Sauce and Choy Sum

This meal will serve two to three people. The following are the ingredients that you need to prepare: 3/4 lbs choy sum sliced into 2 1/2 inch pieces, 1/8 cup plum sauce, 1 tablespoon Chinese rice wine, 3/4 tablespoon soy sauce, 1/2 teaspoon sesame oil, 1/4 cup peanut oil, 1 sliced small onion, 2 finely chopped garlic cloves, 1 teaspoon finely chopped fresh ginger, 1/2 lb pork loin fillet sliced thinly across the grain, 1 tablespoon cornflour seasoned with salt and pepper

Place a large saucepan of lightly salted water over medium heat and bring to a boil. Add the choy sum and cook for 2 minutes, or until stems become crisp yet fork tender. Drain and put under iced water to stop cooking, then drain.

Combine the plum sauce, soy sauce, rice wine, and sesame oil in a non-metallic bowl, then set aside.

Place the wok over high heat and heat 1/2 tablespoon of peanut oil. Reduce heat to medium, then stir fry the garlic, onion, and ginger for 3 minutes. Remove and set aside.

Coat the pork in the seasoned cornflour. Place the wok over high heat and heat the rest of the peanut oil. Cook the pork for 3 minutes or until golden on both sides. Remove and set aside.

Drain the oil from the wok and put back the meat and juices. Add the sauce and stir fry over high heat for 3 minutes, then add the choy sum and the onion mixture. Cook for 2 minutes, then serve immediately.

Chapter 7 – Cleaning your Wok

After a full day's work, it won't be unusual seeing your wok demanding clean-up after producing the most delectable dishes. Making stir-fried chicken and your favorite ramen is no joke. In order for your wok to maintain its beauty and for it to be able to serve you longer, you need to properly maintain it. Note that similar to cast iron skillets, wok that is usually made up of carbon steel requires some tender loving care so you need to master the art of cleaning your wok. Here's the good news, it does not really have to be a complicated thing. You only have to remember three things: (1) rinse, (2) scrub, and (3) dry. For you to not get lost or confused, here's a step-by-step guide that you can always go back to for a better cleaning experience.

When your wok has already experienced cooking many stir-fried and other dishes, your steel wok is able to naturally develop a special seasoned coating that makes it nonstick. This special coat even helps improve the flavor of the next dishes you will cook in it. In order to protect this particular coating, you need to avoid the use of anything that is abrasive when you clean your wok. Therefore, a steel wool is a big no-no. Chemically, it is quite unacceptable to use a cleaning agent that is stronger that dish soap.

Truth be told, veteran wok cooks would not even recommend the used of dish washing liquids and related products. More often than not, hot water is more than enough for washing your wok. Together with a cleaning pad, you can assure that your wok is 100 percent clean. For stubborn and sticky food bits, these can be removed by letting the wok hold the water for a while until the food bits are loose enough.

Once your wok is clean, you may now dry your wok. To do this, all you have to do is to place your wok over low heat until all moisture has evaporated. This step should not be missed because if you store a moist wok, rust can develop. You would not want to have a rusty wok.

Conclusion

Thank you again for purchasing this book!

I hope this book was able to help you to cook the best stir-fried meals and other wok recipes.

The next step is to not take our word for it and trying the Wok recipes for yourself. Have fun and enjoy the good food that we have shared with you.

Finally, if you enjoyed this book, please take the time to share your thoughts and post a review on Amazon. We do our best to reach out to readers and provide the best value we can. Your positive review will help us achieve that. It'd be greatly appreciated!

Thank you and good luck!

Check Out My Other Books

Below you'll find some of my other popular books that are popular on Amazon and Kindle as well. Simply click on the links below to check them out. Alternatively, you can visit my author page on Amazon to see other work done by me.

Ultimate Canning & Preserving Food Guide for Beginners

http://amzn.to/1vwrNVP

Cooking for One Cookbook for Beginners

http://amzn.to/THAD6y

Ultimate Barbecue & Grilling for Beginners

http://amzn.to/VNzsVl

The Ultimate Bread Baking Guide for Beginners

http://amzn.to/VCCzzo

Slow Cooking Guide for Beginners

http://amzn.to/1meo2fi

If the links do not work, for whatever reason, you can simply search for these titles on the Amazon website to find them.

18026206R00038

Printed in Great Britain
by Amazon